A boy named
Mike

PAGE PUBLISHING
Conneaut Lake, PA

First originally published by Page Publishing 2023

ISBN 979-8-88960-929-2 (pbk)
ISBN 979-8-88960-953-7 (digital)

Printed in the United States of America

A boy named Mike

Michael Hensley

Mike was a little boy who grew up in Delaware.
Mike's family was poor, so he didn't always have the nicest things.

At times, people gave food and clothes to Mike's family. His family was on welfare. When Mike was in school, he got free school lunches.

Oftentimes, other kids made fun of Mike, his brother, and sister because they didn't always have the cool stuff.

Mike was from a divorced home, with very little money but lots of love.

When Mike was in the fourth grade, he started homeschooling.

As Mike grew, he knew he wanted to do something different. Mike knew he wanted to serve in some way. He often dreamed of being a cop.

Mike worked many farm-related jobs while homeschooling.

When Mike was sixteen years old, he completed high school and started college.

Even though Mike was working and going to college, he dreamed of doing more.

When Mike turned eighteen, he decided to join the Marine Corps.

While serving as a Marine, Mike did many things. He went to boot camp.

He lived in many different states: North Carolina, South Carolina, Tennessee, Hawaii, and Virginia

He went to many places throughout the world: Okinawa, Italy, Greece, Spain, Liberia, Ukraine, Thailand, Iraq, and several other countries.

Mike got to do cool things like live on a Navy ship, travel around the world, and visit historic places like Florence and Pompeii in Italy.

Throughout his time in the Marine Corps, Mike got married to Tiffany, had children, and went back to school.

Mike had six kids and two fur babies. Their names were Anthony, Lee-Ann, Jacob, Ava, Izzy, Juli, Jaxon and Isla.

He had many jobs in the Marine Corps and worked at several different places:

Marine Aviation Logistics Squadron 29,

Second Air Naval Gunfire Liaison Company,

Marine Corps Base Quantico,

Education Command and Marine Corps University, and

United States Naval Community College.

And then Mike got selected to serve as the director of the Marine Corps Senior Enlisted Academy.

24

Mike constantly emphasizes to people, "It is not about where you start in life because you decide where you finish."

Eventually, Mike's family was able to purchase a home in Spotsylvania, Virginia.

After years of serving as a United States Marine, Mike made it to a level of responsibility very few Marines attain. All this despite growing up poor, from a divorced home, and often being called stupid.

Mike wants everyone to know that it's not where you start in life that matters; you can achieve your dreams.

Never let anyone define you, including yourself, by how or where you grew up. You have no boundaries and can achieve anything you decide to do. You have endless potential.

About the Author

 Mike grew up in Delaware, in the small town of Laurel. The challenges faced by Mike growing up are also faced by many children, and Mike wants them to know they can succeed. Throughout his career in the Marine Corps, Mike has had many adventures and seen many countries. These adventures included the ability to attend college and complete his degrees, which led him to start his doctorate. Mike loves his family, his country, and God, and this is why he loves serving his country and wants to positively impact the lives of children. Mike wants every child to know they have the ability to achieve greatness.

Printed in the USA
CPSIA information can be obtained
at www.ICGtesting.com
LVHW060730100124
768547LV00089B/2780